FLASHCARD BOOKS
ANIMALS
ENGLISH to RUSSIAN
FLASHCARD BOOK

BLACK & WHITE EDITION

HOW TO USE:

- READ THE ENGLISH WORD ON THE FIRST PAGE.

- IF YOU KNOW THE TRANSLATION SAY IT OUT LOUD.

- TURN THE PAGE AND SEE IF YOU GOT IT RIGHT.

- IF YOU GUESSED CORRECTLY, WELL DONE!
IF NOT, TRY READING THE WORD USING THE PHONETIC PRONUNCIATION GUIDE.

- NOW TRY THE NEXT PAGE.
THE MORE YOU PRACTICE THE BETTER YOU WILL GET!

BOOKS IN THIS SERIES:
ANIMALS
NUMBERS SHAPES AND COLORS
HOUSEHOLD ITEMS
CLOTHES

ALSO AVAILABLE IN OTHER LANGUAGES INCLUDING:

FRENCH, GERMAN, SPANISH, ITALIAN,

RUSSIAN, CHINESE, JAPANESE AND MORE.

WWW.FLASHCARDEBOOKS.COM

Bat

Летучая мышь

Le-tU-cha-ya mysh

Bear

Медведь

Myed-vYEd'

Bee

Пчела

Pche-LA

Bull

Бык

Вук

Butterfly

Бабочка

BA-bach-ka

Cat

Кошка

KOsh-ka

Cheetah

Гепард

Ge-pArd

Chicken

Курица

KU-ri-tsa

Корова

Ka-rO-va

Crab

Краб

Krab

Crocodile

Крокодил

Kra-ka-dIL

Dog

Собака

Sa-bA-ka

Dolphin

Дельфин

Del'-fln

Deer

Олень

O-LYEn'

Слон

Slon

Fish

Рыба

RY-ba

Flamingo

Фламинго

Fla-mIn-go

Fox

Лиса

Li-sA

Frog

Лягушка

Lya-gUsh-ka

Giraffe

Жираф

Zhi-rAf

Goat

Коза

Ka-zA

Goose

Гусь

Gus'

Gorilla

Горилла

Ga-rl-la

Hamster

Хомяк

Ha-mYAk

Hippo

Бегемот

Be-ge-mOt

Horse

Лошадь

LO-shad'

Iguana

Игуана

I-gu-A-na

Jellyfish

Медуза

Me-dU-za

Kangaroo

Кенгуру

Ken-gu-rU

Koala

Коала

Ko-A-la

Lady bird

Божья коровка

BO-zh'ya ka-rOv-ka

Lion

Лев

Lyev

Manatee

Морская корова

Mar-skA-ya ka-rO-va

Monkey

Обезьяна

A-be-z'YA-na

Mouse

Мышь

Mysh

Ostrich

Страус

StrA-us

Owl

Сова

Sa-vA

Panda

Панда

PAn-da

Parakeet

Волнистый попугай
Val-nIs-tyi pa-pu-gAy

Parrot

Попугай

Pa-pu-gAy

Penguin

Пингвин

Pin-gvIn

Pig

Свинья

Svi-n'YA

Pigeon

Голубь

GO-lup'

Rabbit

Кролик

KrO-lik

Rat

Крыса

KrY-sa

Носорог
Na-sa-rOg

Rooster

Петух

Pe-tUh

Scorpion

Скорпион

Skar-pi-On

Seagull

Чайка

ChAy-ka

Seal

Тюлень

Tu-LEn'

Shark

Акула

A-kU-la

Sheep

Овца

Af-tsA

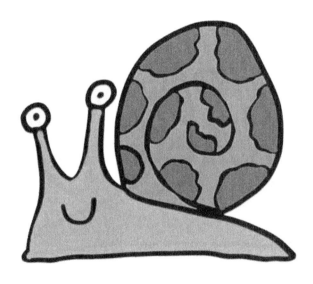

Snail

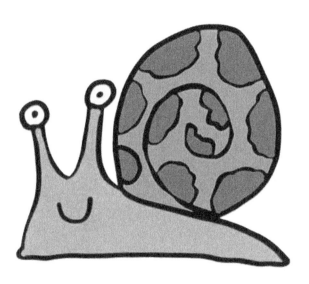

Улитка

U-LI-tka

Snake

Змея

Zme-YA

Squirrel

Белка

BEl-ka

Stag

Олень

Alyen'

Stork

Аист

A-ist

Tiger

Тигр
Tigr

Toad

Жаба

ZhA-ba

Черепаха

Che-re-pA-ha

Turkey

Индейка

In-dEy-ka

Turtle

Морская черепаха

Mar-skA-ya che-re-pA-ha

Wolf

Волк

Volk

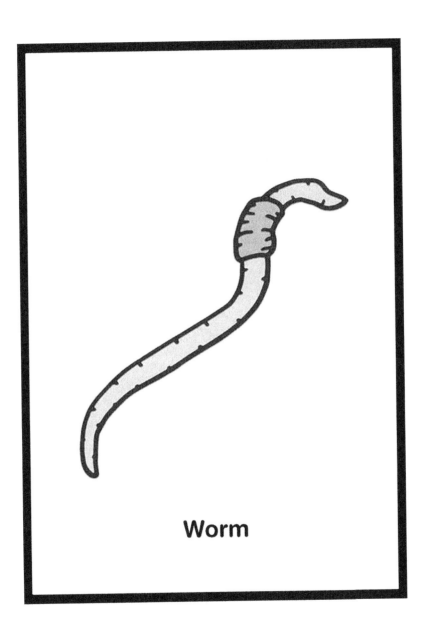

Worm

Червь

Cherf'

ALL IMAGES COPYRIGHT ANTONY BRIGGS 2017

if you have enjoyed this book, please leave an Amazon review.

Thanks

CPSIA information can be obtained
at www.ICGtesting.com
Printed in the USA
BVOW06s1353211217
503315BV00040B/2579/P